DECEPTION

ROBERT C. PATUTO

DECEPTION

Robert C. Patuto

Logos to Rhema Publishers
Tulsa, Oklahoma

Deception
Copyright © 2011 Robert C. Patuto

All rights reserved. No portion of this book may be reproduced, stored in a retrieval system, or transmitted in any form or by any means—electronic, mechanical, photocopy, recording, scanning, or other—except for brief quotations in critical reviews or articles, without the prior written permission of the author, Phyllis Hill, or the publisher, Logos to Rhema Publishing, except as provided by United States of America copyright law.

Unless otherwise noted,
all Scripture quotations are from:

The King James Version of the Bible

Scripture taken from the New King James Version.
Copyright 1982 by Thomas Nelson, Inc.
Used by permission. All rights reserved.

Scripture taken from the New American Standard Bible, Copyright 1960, 1962, 1963, 1968, 1971,1973,1975, 1977, 1995,
by the Lockman Foundation.
Used by permission.

ISBN 13: 978-1461107507
ISBN 10: 1461107504

Published in the
United States of America by
Susan K. Reidel
LOGOS TO RHEMA PUBLISHERS
7822 E 100th Street
Tulsa, OK 74133
(918) 606-5346

Publisher Website: logostorhema.com
Publisher e-mail: sreidel@hotmail.com

About the Author

Robert C. Patuto

The author's background is forty-two years in the hotel and resort industry within the United States, Mexico, and off shore resorts.

Robert C. Patuto was involved in the operations of three hundred and fifty hotels within forty-four states. What he observed was that deceptions were running rampant in this field of work.

The writing is timely, as the world is becoming global and travel and living abroad and away from home is a reality of our present day.

As you read this information it will profit you in the future years to come. You will not only benefit from the observation of the writings but you will clearly understand the reasons of the writing of this book, Deception.

Contents

Forward		9
Author's note to the reader		11
Chapter One	Deception	13
Chapter Two	The Holy Spirit	19
Chapter Three	Boston	27
Chapter Four	Dr. Lester Sumrall	35
Chapter Five	The God of this World	43
Chapter Six	The Word	49
Chapter Seven	Satan, the Enemy of God	55
Chapter Eight	Lucifer	61
Chapter Nine	The Choice of Angels	69

FOREWORD
BY
Dr. LESTER SUMRALL

It is a pleasure for me to recommend Robert Patuto. We have known him personally for several years and observed his experiences in the gospel.

He is well qualified to discuss the subject at hand. Deception has a prophetic significance, especially for these last days. Robert has had such unusual experiences with business leaders and religious leaders, that he understands how easily one can be deceived if he does not have a mind centered in Christ.

I trust that these words are an inspiration to you as a reader and it will be a guide to obey the words of God which teach us not to believe every spirit, but to test them by the Word of God. May the Lord guide you in His truth.

IMPORTANT THOUGHT

Please do not speed read this book. Read carefully especially all the Scriptures. Pray for the Holy Spirit to assist you to understand these writings. Satan will do anything to keep you from the understanding of this series. Pray that the spirit of confusion be bound. First John 4:4 says, "Greater is he that is in you than he that is in the world."

Remember victory is our goal.

Chapter 1

CHAPTER ONE

DECEPTION

Deception...the very fact that the word exists and is used causes distress, the fear of being on the deceived end, a realization! It is talked about on a surface level, but to spread its total contents on a buffet table would present revelations to most, and would have varied effects on many believers as well as unbelievers. Denominations, in concert, would object to the existence of a good majority of the very simple deceptions in the world, to say nothing of the more complex. The Scriptures definitely warn of deception:

> "Behold, I send you forth as sheep in the midst of wolves; be ye therefore wise as serpents and harmless as doves (or as innocent as doves)." Matthew 10:16

The subject of deception, from the beginning of the world to the final days in the Book of Revelation, is mentioned sparingly in many Christian books, written and totally overlooked or brushed under the carpet by some pastors, priests, preachers, Jewish teachers, and evangelists of the diversified ministries. There are a number of the above that briefly discuss it, yet paradoxically these teach little or nothing of the fathoms deception covers and its devastating consequences.

This book will cover multiple levels, beginning with the first deception on record, including compound deceptions, and ultimately, the final deceptions prophesied. Some of us will be appalled at the fact that we (believers) could possibly be deceived daily in our walk with the Lord.

The purpose of this book is to alert believers by exposing the enemy and to provoke the army of the Lord (you and me) to perceive the adversary's unending, inexhaustible list of deceptions. Write this verse in the front of your mind: "Neither give place to the devil…" Ephesians 4:27 and carve this one into your innermost being: "For the weapons of our warfare are not carnal, but mighty through God to the pulling down of strongholds, casting down imaginations and every highly thing that exalteth itself against the knowledge of God, and bringing into captivity every thought to the obedience of Christ." I Corinthians 10:3-4

Webster's definition of deception is *something that deceives, a trick, as an illusion, or is meant to deceive, as a fraud or imposter, a counterfeit.* Sound familiar? Revelation 12:9 declares, "And the great dragon was cast out, that old serpent called the devil and Satan which deceiveth the whole world." He was cast out into the earth and his angels were cast out with him.

The main thrust of this book on deception is to assist the believer in obtaining total victory. This is only accomplishable through total commitment, and an awareness of the adversary which will assist you in reaching that total commitment.

The Lord spoke through Paul regarding deception in Ephesians 4:17-19, "This I say, therefore, and testify in the Lord that ye henceforth walk not as other Gentiles walk in the vanity (or emptiness) of their mind, having their understanding darkened, being alienated from the life of God through the ignorance that is in them because of the blindness of their heart." That's a lack of knowledge of deception. "Who being past feeling have given themselves over unto lasciviousness, to work all uncleanness and greediness."

Chapter 2

CHAPTER TWO

THE HOLY SPIRIT

The Holy Spirit indwells every believer. The believer may be immature, but if he has been born again, the Holy Spirit dwells in him. It is one thing for us to have the Holy Spirit dwelling in us, but, does the Holy Spirit have you, that He may fill you with abundant life which will protect you against deceptions of the adversary? You may be filled with the Holy Spirit many times; not once, filled, always filled, (which is another deception).

The apostles who were filled in Acts chapter 2, were filled again in chapter 4. And to be filled with the Holy Spirit is to be Spirit possessed. Let's go back to you, the believer when you made a decision to be born again into the Kingdom of the Lord, you were transformed, changed by the power of God; conformed to the perfect will of God, to live abundantly. The abundant life is a separated life. You have been separated unto the gospel of God. As Paul states in Romans 1:1, we are "...servant(s) of Jesus Christ...separated unto the gospel of God," and we have made the same decision that Joshua made in his book chapter 24:15, "Choose you this day whom ye will serve..." (we've made that decision) "...whether the gods which your fathers served that were on the other side of the flood, or the gods of the Amorites, in whose land ye dwell, but as for me and my house we will serve the Lord."

At that moment, it may have been one-half hour ago or twenty years ago, you should have drawn a line of demarcation. You chose sides. There are only two sides, God's or His adversary, Satan. You should have known at that time that by making this commitment to Jesus Christ you can now have fellowship with God. That's the best deal in the world, having fellowship with your Creator.

Therefore, by making this decision to follow Jesus Christ we have been transformed and changed by the power of God. A new life has been started. You are no longer conformed to this world. Now you can be conformed to the perfect will of God and live abundantly. But the abundant life is, as I said, a separated life. Separated from what? God demands (He doesn't request) separation from the world,

Satan's system. Don't be deceived here, making this decision was a meaningful act of self-discipline. You put on the other side of this new life, your former identity, giving up the old life. Galatians 2:20 says, "I am crucified with Christ; nevertheless I live; yet not I, but Christ liveth in me; and the life which I now live in the flesh I live by the faith of the Son of God, who loved me, and gave himself for me." Hebrews 12:1 tells us that we should"...lay aside every weight, and the sin which doth so easily beset us, and let us run with patience the race that is set before us."

Back to separation, 2 Corinthians 6:14, "Be ye not unequally yoked together with unbelievers: for what fellowship hath righteousness with unrighteousness? And what communion hath light with darkness? And what concord hath Christ with Belial? Or what part hath he that believeth with an infidel? And what agreement hath the temple of God with idols? For ye are the temple of the living God: as God hath said, I will dwell in them, and walk in them; and I will be their God, and they shall be my people. Wherefore come out from among them, and be ye separate..." That doesn't sound like a request, but a command. Second Corinthians 7:1 tells us, "Having therefore these promises, dearly beloved, let us cleanse ourselves from all filthiness of the flesh and spirit, perfecting holiness in the fear of God." There are volumes of situations involving Christians who have married non-Christians, gone into business or associated socially with unbelievers. Most end up with problems. Many believe they'll love them and get them on the "salvation trail." There are a few cases of some getting saved, but you put yourself in Satan's territory and cannot expect God's blessings on such a union, because it is contrary to His Word. In the majority of cases, the believer is pulled down to the level of the unbeliever. From a business outlook it's a major risk spiritually. By being unequally yoked, you are keeping God out of your partnership.

The orthodox Jews (those who followed the law) knew the consequences of being unequally yoked. They heard Jehovah, Deuteronomy 7:2-4, "...thou shalt make no covenant with them, nor shew mercy unto them; Neither shalt thou make marriages with them; thy daughter thou shalt not give unto his son, nor his daughter shalt thou take unto thy son. For they will turn away thy son from following me, that they may serve other gods; so will the anger of the Lord be kindled against you, and destroy thee suddenly."

The Lord got His message through with clarity. We become concerned why our prayers have not been answered, why we cannot have total victory, why we are in bondage. We have been faithful. Loved our brethren and…let's see what the Lord says in Isaiah 59:1, "Behold, the Lord's hand is not shortened, that it cannot save; neither his ear heavy, that it cannot hear. But your iniquities have separated between you and your God, and your sins have hid his face from you, that he will not hear. For your hands are defiled with blood, and your fingers with iniquity; your lips have spoken lies, your tongue hath uttered perverseness." The definition of iniquity is a wicked, unjust or unrighteous act, or an act of deceit.

Chapter 3

Chapter Three

Boston

Growing up in the Boston area during the 1940's, 1950's, and 1960's as a Roman Catholic attending Roman Catholic schools, I was getting involved in the church as an altar boy and had aspirations to attend the seminary to become a priest. I unfortunately did not associate with people of the Jewish faith whatsoever. It was forbidden to enter any non-Catholic institution of prayer. This directive still exists in certain areas of the world in the Catholic religion. Nationalities lived in specific areas with each other. The majority of the Italians lived in the Back Bay area, the Irish in the Dorchester area, Chinese in Chinatown, Jews in the Brookline Newton area, and African Americans in the Roxbury section of Boston. My belief is that if God had designed, or intended these divisions because of doctrines and customs, He would have sectioned off the United States and informed us. The loss of education and sharing caused from this segregation was astronomical, even up to today!

As a second-generation Italian, I was raised on an additional set of Ten Commandments, being warned about all the negatives of all the nationalities. It appeared that my nationality had presented itself with a clean bill of health. You could socialize with these other nationalities, but you were to watch them closely so as not to be deceived. This list grew as more and more foreigners entered the country. For all of our general information, these foreigners were led to the United States of America in God's plan, I believe, for this "Christian" nation to witness to them. Some came here for religious freedom to worship God, to improve their lifestyle and to get away from oppressive governments. There are certain believers who are still condemning our government for letting them in, along with putting down these people for who they think they are and for their customs. This is judging and deception. These foreigners have always needed Jesus, and still do need Jesus. Those we don't win to Christ will ultimately become our enemies. We have the opportunity to witness and win them to the Kingdom of the living God; if we are operating in and led by the Holy Spirit.

Miss Emma Lazarus, a Russian Jew (Zionist) wrote the great entrance sign into New York harbor (U.S.A.) called the New Colossus, on the Statue of Liberty. She wrote, "Give me your tired, your poor, your huddled masses yearning to breathe free; the wretched refuse of your teeming shores; send these, the homeless, tempest-tossed to me. I lift my lamp beside the Golden Door." We could have added to that several Scriptures. Being a Jew, Zionist she might have related to part of them. My Scripture selection would be, "If the Son therefore shall make you free you shall be free indeed," John 8:36. The definition of free is liberty, but we ignorant believers have assisted in the oppression of foreigners. We're still judging by appearance and culture, a deception of the devil, and believers are falling into it.

Getting back to my neighborhood, the interesting item is that no one ever told us to watch out for the devil, for he was and is in all the nationalities deceiving humanity.

1 Peter 5:8 tells us to "Be sober, be vigilant (watchful); because your adversary, the devil, as a roaring lion, walketh about, seeking whom he may (has permission to) devour." He's already looking for the deceived, because hunting lions don't roar. He's headed for the prey that is

already deceived, so Peter is telling us to get our act together and our spiritual eyes opened; to stay sober and vigilant.

The hotel industry is a unique field, for you who are not familiar with it. It offers a certain amount of glamour even at the lowest end of the organizational chart. Even positions such as waiter, busboy, bartender, room clerk, bellman, etc., tend to be glamorous. Advertisements for hotel correspondence schools create a deceptive view to someone considering changing fields of endeavor. Through the early stages of my career in the hotel industry as a dishwasher and through the various positions all the way to the top there lay a great sequence of opportunities to be deceptive, ways of buying better positions. Theft runs the gamut in the hotel industry theft of anything you can possibly pick up, china, glasses, silver, foodstuffs, tips, and so on; guestroom thefts by security, maids, and management. Yes, the deception of eliminating management from suspicion of theft leaves many unanswered insurance claims...cash shortages, checks sent to companies that do not exist for merchandise that never arrives, checks sent to counterfeit travel agencies who become partners with top-level management; percentage checks from vending machines that never appear on the P&L statements, adding to millions of dollars. Not a believer until 1975, I was seventeen years into the business which led me to be deceived my many situations and to be the deceiver in many situations.

Chapter 4

CHAPTER FOUR

DR. LESTER SUMRALL

I was miraculously saved at the Tri-County Assembly of God in Cincinnati, Ohio in 1975 on Palm Sunday. Although saved and a new creature, the enemy does not waste any time in coming in to try to steal the seed, as many of us have experienced. I did not get into the Word of God as I should. Why? It was not emphasized. We believers are guilty, Cervantes says, "...forewarned is forearmed." I didn't choose to have the proper fellowship with believers, and because of these things, I was ultimately weakened. By 1978, three years later, the destroyer of families was working triple-time. Divorce seemed inevitable, for I had left God and joined forces with the enemy, deceived by personal glory and pride. Deeply involved with the world, I was operating five hotels and a fashionable discotheque in Dallas.

Shortly after I left my family, I lost my position of three years, never zeroing in on one of the most important quotations of our Lord in Matthew 26:41, "Watch and pray that ye enter not into temptation. The spirit indeed is willing, but the flesh is weak." My flesh was weak. After the realization that I had fallen from the grace of God, I sought counseling. I was overcome seriously and oppressed by a spirit of fear, anxiety, depression and guilt; all works of deceptions by the adversary.

But these deceptions backfired, bringing me to my knees to ask the Lord for His perfect will in my life. Making this volitional surrender to the Word of God, even though I didn't know God's perfect will, was an act of faith on my part. Romans 12:2 tells us not to be conformed to this world but "...be ye transformed by the renewing of your mind, that ye may prove what is that good and acceptable and perfect will of God." Your whole man, spirit, soul and body was redeemed on Calvary and sanctified. We are to present our bodies as a living sacrifice.

A new job opened up as of January 1981 when I was requested to work on a hotel rehabilitation program for multiple hotels, beginning with a project in northern Indiana in the South Bend area of the state. I fought the situation, I did not want to go, but the promises behind it and the fact that it would only last six weeks. I accepted and arrived on the seventh day of January. However, due to my depressed state, fear was overtaking all. I relocated the managing quarters of this particular hotel into a suite, not wanting to deal with the mundane situations of the hotel operations. I diligently set up a rehabilitation program the first week, hoping to get out of town quick, but the Lord had a plan that lasted four months in northern Indiana.

It began one snowy, cold, miserable, lonely, typical, mid-western winter night when I was buried in my suite with the heat blasting for security, watching cable television. I was thoroughly convinced that even though I had requested the perfect will of God, that God had made His first mistake (not knowing immediately why God had sent me from 71-degree temperatures in Dallas to 15-degree weather in South Bend, Indiana).

That evening on cable television a preacher caught my attention as quick as lightning, and I began to take notes on a subject I had never heard of, *Where Was God When Pagan Religions Began?* When this preacher finished his sermon, he introduced himself and informed everyone of the location of his church (which I was able to figure out after I had enjoyed this fantastic program), was only ten minutes from the hotel. The Lord, in His divine planning, (via cable television) had introduced me to Dr. Lester Sumrall and put me in the back yard of his church.

This began a new relationship with the Lord, knowing what was required to put me back on course. Within two weeks I was involved not only with Dr. Sumrall's church and family, but with the Full Gospel Business Men's Fellowship International in the South Bend area. During that period of time I received for the first time the strength of the Baptism of the Holy ghost as is described in Acts 2:4, "...and they were all filled with the Holy Ghost and began to speak in other tongues, as the Spirit gave them utterance." Jesus, through Dr. Sumrall (within a week) delivered me from fear, oppression, anxiety, depression and whoever else happened to be hanging around in my life. God miraculously used Dr. Sumrall as His instrument in my life.

This supernatural introduction via TV was not only to Dr. Sumrall, but to an evangelist that I did not appreciate nor even like, at that time (attitudes). I was introduced that evening to Kenneth Copeland immediately following Dr. Sumrall's program.

The Lord truly has some interesting methods of introductions and placing you with people you would never in years believe.

Following four months with Dr. Sumrall (six weeks were originally planned) training in

God's army, getting involved in Christian TV Channel 46 in South Bend, and speaking to his congregation and to the Full Gospel Business Men in the South Bend and Rockford, Illinois areas, to youth groups about the evils of disco and rock music (all the devil's territory), I returned to Dallas a new man and believe this, I found it difficult to leave South Bend, Indiana!

My son, Michael, joined me for his spring vacation the year of 1981 in South Bend and while he was there he rededicated his life to the Lord and is now actively serving the Lord in various areas. During this four-month period, God mended all situations and put me in a greater position what Satan planned for evil, God turned around for good and His Glory!

Chapter 5

Chapter Five

The God of this World

Let's go further into this subject of deception, a subject that we consider to be of a most serious nature. We are now entering upon the foundation for the god of this world. Second Corinthians 4:4 says, "In whom the god of this world hath blinded the minds of them which believe not, lest the light of the glorious gospel of Christ, who is the image of god, should shine unto them." The power of the enemy (yours and mine) is being highlighted as a profitable study. Every believer is a soldier in God's army. If you are to set up a standard for success in spiritual warfare against this totally evil, diabolical enemy, you must know his history and his complete makeup. Cast out and destroy, all teaching which states there is no evil leader behind the evil that exists today. Some preachers don't teach it and don't want to hear about it, but here it is, engrave it into your memory. Some pastors and their congregations feel that centering on the subject of man's enemy (Satan) is spiritually unhealthy and they quote such statements as, "If we look to the Lord and have faith, this concentration on the enemy is not required."

The enemy (Satan) is constantly concentrating on God's creation, as 1 Peter 5:8 points out. Christians or believers, ignorant of his devices, will be defeated. That's very simple. Isaiah 5:13 says, "Therefore my people are gone into captivity, because they have no knowledge; and their honorable men are famished, and their multitude dried up with thirst. Therefore hell hath enlarged herself, and opened her mouth without measure: and their glory, and their multitude, and their pomp, and he that rejoiceth, shall descend into it." That's fairly simple; we are in warfare.

It's amazing, we can participate in sporting events and business competition and we all realize that the most important function of sporting participation and competition in business is to know the opposition. For example, in baseball, it's how they hit, run, field, pitch, etc. In business competition it's what is their market and product? How good is their product, and do they have a better mousetrap?

Yet, as believers we leave out the fact that we must know the competitor of competitors and the opposition of oppositions (Satan). Hosea 4:6, "My people are destroyed for lack of knowledge. As thou hast rejected knowledge, I will also reject thee, that thou shalt be no priest to me, seeing thou hast forgotten the law of thy God I will also forget their children."

Brother and sister, rejecting the Lord is joining the enemy, any form of rejection! One form of rejection is not following God's commands and one of His greatest commands is to put on the whole armor of God that we might be protected against the wiles of the devil" (Ephesians 6:11-18). Second Peter 1:5-10 says, "And beside this, giving all diligence, add to your faith virtue; and to virtue knowledge, and to knowledge temperance; and to temperance patience; and to patience godliness; And to godliness brotherly kindness; and to brotherly kindness, charity (love). For if these things be in you, and abound, they make you that ye shall neither be barren nor unfruitful in the knowledge of our Lord Jesus Christ. But he that lacketh these things is blind, and cannot see afar off, and hath forgotten that he was purged from his old sins. Wherefore the rather, brethren, giving diligence to make your calling and election sure: for if ye do these things, ye shall never fall."

God is not double-minded. James 1:8 tells us that a double-minded man is unstable in all his ways. There are zero gray areas in the Kingdom of God. Many business dealings in the non-Christian as well as in the believer's world lie in constant gray areas. If you are dealing in those gray areas, clean up your act or face the consequences.

"Oh, don't worry about that invoice, good old Brother James will write it off." This is one of the reasons some of the good old brethren are becoming poor witnesses, by going out of business, and of course, you know it's not scriptural for a brother in the Lord to sue or take another to court so they try to take advantage of him through their deliberate dishonesty.

Income taxes, alimony, paying your bills in general, all can be traps in the web of Satan. Wheeling and dealing by fellow-Christians and non-Christians is also a trap where a deal may look good to you but is really not that good for the consumer. The Lord has told us not to be lukewarm, to be either hot or cold, or He will spew us out of His mouth.

"Submit yourselves, therefore, to God. Resist the devil and he will flee from you." You cannot resist unless your are trained and protected with the full armor of God. Draw nigh to God and He'll draw nigh to you. Cleanse your hands of all bad business dealings, you sinners, and purify your hearts, ye double-minded.

Chapter 6

Chapter Six

The Word

As the influence of Satan increases, we will see a departure from the true faith. Hold fast, let no man steal your crown (or your reward). Quoting John G. Lake, "A holy mind cannot repeat a vile thing, nor be the creator of such an act." I say with Paul, "...mark them which cause divisions and offences contrary to the doctrine which ye have learned; and avoid them" Romans 16:17, (NIV). He may talk, but he does not know God. He does not comprehend the power of salvation nor is he the possessor of the Holy Spirit.

The only way we learn about our enemy is through the word. Satan, our adversary, hates the Bible because it blows his cover and most denominations work with him i.e., God's Word is not taught and practiced in its revelation and power. Therefore he is able to work behind the scenes, which is a major deception.

We have a formidable foe. Make this clear in our mind. We are not in a position to take elusive shots at our enemy and his forces. Which is an area that many pastors should monitor more closely in their ministries, especially youth ministries, that are railing accusations against the devil. Number one, they will not move Satan or his company and it can and has been proven to provide devastating consequences to people who insist on taking shots at him. For example, on the dispute over Moses' body, "Yet Michael the archangel, when contending with the devil he disputed about the body of Moses, durst not bring against him a railing accusation, but said, The Lord rebuke thee," Jude 9. Jesus, in His confrontations in Matthew 4:4,7 and 10, used abrupt but sound rebuke, using the Word as a sword with instant results. In Matthew 4:4 when Jesus was tempted of Satan His answer was immediate, "It is written, man shall not live by bread alone, but by every word that proceeded out of the mouth of God." Did Satan quit then? No, immediately in verse 5 he takes Him up into the holy city and setteth Him on a pinnacle of the temple and again tempted Him. Jesus said to him in verse 7, "It is written again, thou shalt not tempt the Lord thy God." Did the devil quit?? Let's see. In verse 9 he took Him up to an exceedingly high mountain and showed Him the world at a glance and offered it to him if He would bow down and worship Him. In verse 10 Jesus used the word, "Get thee hence, Satan, for it is written thou shalt worship the Lord thy God and Him only shalt thou serve." Then Satan left him for a season. After Jesus used the Word three times against three temptations or possible deceptions, the devil split. Hallelujah!

Now if Satan attacked Jesus, the divine Son of God three times why do we think he'll only attack us once, and when we bind him he'll never come back? Instead of binding him, use the Word. There's nothing wrong with binding him, but use the Word. Please take note so that you are not deceived, that although authority has most definitely been passed down to us through Christ, there were no additional mandates giving us additional elementary verbiage to be spoken to the enemy and his company. Use the Word of God. The apostle Paul informs us in 2 Corinthians 12:10 "...for when I am weak, then am I strong." Strong in what? Strong in the Lord, strong in the Word, to assist, protect, to discern deceit and counterfeits. If you are strong in the Word you always have the Word with which to defeat the enemy. The impartation of strength comes from the Word.

Again, let me emphasize that this book was written to awaken a sleepy body and inform them as to why so many are in bondage to certain situations, not getting answers to their prayers; we must discern the enemy! Second Corinthians 4:4 informs us, "In whom the god of this world hath blinded the minds of them which believe not, lest the light of the glorious gospel of Christ (who is the image of God) should shine unto them." That's telling us that Satan, the god of this world, consistently blinds the minds of people and fights God's system. He tries in every manner possible to keep the Bible away from the unbelievers. Therefore, without the full armor of God we cannot set up a strategy accordingly and we become deceived and temporarily defeated.

CHAPTER 7

CHAPTER SEVEN

SATAN, THE ENEMY OF GOD

This planet belonged to man from the beginning. Romans 5:17 says that because of one man's offense (Adam's), death reigned in the world. Satan, formerly Lucifer, became the god of this planet through this one sin. Satan has numerous aliases. He is also known to the universe as the devil (little god). John 8:44 says that he is a liar and the father of lies. Mark 3:22 says he's the prince of demons. John 12:31 says he is the prince of the power of the air. Ephesians 2:2 he is called the tempter. Matthew 4:3 he is the serpent; he's known as Beelzebub, and many other names.

He can, if he chooses, disguise himself as an angel of light, which he does constantly at different times and in different ways. Second Corinthians 11:14 enlightens us that it is not unusual for false apostles, prophets, and deceitful workers, to present themselves as followers of Christ. Satan is the master deceiver, and the first one deceived. All these designations refer to a powerful being, the enemy of God who seeks to promote evil, using great cunning to deceive men (the unwary), both the believer and the unbeliever.

Satan, is not the opposite of God, he is the enemy of God. He has been cast out of heaven, doomed eternally, and he has only the power God has allowed him to have and for the period of time in God's timetable. Isaiah 14:12, "How art thou fallen from heaven, O Lucifer, son of the morning! How art thou cut down to the ground, which didst weaken the nations! For thou hast said in thine heart, I will ascend into heaven, I will exalt my throne above the stars of God...I will ascend above the heights of the clouds; I will be like the most High. Yet thou shalt be brought down to hell, to the sides of the pit." He was cast out into the earth and his angels were cast out with him. The Bible says he is now the prince of the power of the air or the prince of this world (Ephesians 2:2; 1 Corinthians 2:8).

The Lord wants us to be aware that our battle is with supernatural powers; and that's every battle we encounter. Ephesians 6:12 says, "For we wrestle not against flesh and blood, but against principalities, against powers, against the rulers of the darkness of this world, against spiritual wickedness in high places." Take a good look at this situation. You can say, "I'm saved, filled with the Holy host, speaking in tongues, and if I can hold off long enough, maybe hide in a corner of my society, I'll avoid the world and go to heaven. Deceived? Yes! Get into the Word it is your strength to do the battle and defeat Satan in your life (Matthew 4:17-19).

Chapter 8

Chapter Eight

Lucifer

The Bible informs us that in the beginning, Genesis 1:1, before the creation of the earth, our enemy whom we know today as Satan, was named Lucifer. The meaning of his name is the light bearer, son of the morning. This was his original state. What a glorious position! Remember that God was, is and always will be in complete control. Nothing in the universe can win over anything of His purpose. God, in the eons of time, before the creation of Lucifer (one of the first creations), stored up or filed away for instant recall, all the would-be names of His creatures. He gave each of His created beings a definition. Now they were innumerable as the stars in the sky and the sand on the shores. I am sure there was great council over these definitions. In God's master plan, He also stored up and has knowledge of all the possibilities of deception, along with a method of suppressing or annihilating them.

So God, being all-knowing, there was nothing throughout eternity that could come as a surprise to Him, nor could anything even be conjured up to defeat His will. Nothing exists in the universe that He didn't create. He created a form of repentance and a method of salvation. Thus, from the beginning of all things prevailed, divine goodness. Everything was good. We have learned from the Word that "God is light and in him is no darkness," John 1:5. James 1:17 tells us, "Every good gift and every perfect gift is from above, and cometh down from the Father of lights, with whom is no variableness neither shadow of turning."

At an appointed time Elohim decided to begin creation in the heavens. It was His desire to populate the heavens for fellowship. Genesis 1:1 tells us that in the beginning God created the heavens and the earth. God, Triune, Father, Word and Spirit (John 1:1). Genesis 1:2 makes us aware that God created darkness, which was a part of the creation, and He wasn't totally satisfied so He sent the Holy Spirit upon the face of the deep (indicating the earth, because the earth was total water). Remember, God is light. Jesus is light, and God sent His Holy Spirit way back in Genesis 1:2, as He does now (to brood over chaotic life on earth). He begins to perfect His new creation, that's us, to bring forth order out of chaos, where we may see the splendor of Shekinah.

God created every thing, the heavens, the earth on the first day. He simply said, "Let there be light," on the earth light had been from the beginning of time. God being light, (God has always been and always will be). As soon as the words were enunciated, there was light on the earth and, seeing that it was good, He created division between light and darkness. The light that God sent to earth at the beginning is not the same as the light emitted by the sun, the moon and the stars, which bodies did not appear until the fourth day of creation. The light on the first day was a sort that would have enabled man to see the world at a glance (God's glory) and we know that Jesus was, is, and always will be that light. John 12 reads, "I am the light of the world; he that followed me shall not walk in darkness but shall have the light of life." Because of the wickedness of a sinful generation of man (as we stated before, nothing comes as a surprise to God), man was unworthy to enjoy the blessings of such Shekinah light, so God concealed it. But in Revelation 21:23 it reappears in all its pristine glory. "And the city had no need of the sun, neither of the moon to shine in; for the glory of God did lighten it and the Lamb is the light thereof. Perhaps during this interim between Genesis 1:1 and 1:3 there was a requirement for a light bearer, or a light giver (Latin context) of heaven. As we read in Colossians 1:16 Jesus created everything: "For by Him were all things created that are in heaven and that are in earth, visible and invisible, whether they be thrones or dominions or principalities or powers, all things were created by him and for him."

We relate back to the order of angels, and verse 17 says, "And he is before all things and by him all things consist." The great commission created a great archangel, for a purpose, a holy being, looking into the massive library of definitions they find the definition "light bearer" to be the description of the name "Lucifer, who was a masterpiece creation. Scripture informs us in Ezekiel 28:14 that Lucifer was a sinless and righteous being. Ezekiel 28:12-13 tells us (referring to Lucifer), "...thou sealest up the sum, full of wisdom and perfect beauty. Thou hast been in Eden, the garden of God. Every precious stone was their covering, the sardius, topaz and the diamond, the beryl, the onyx and the jasper; the sapphire, the emerald and the carbuncle and gold. The workmanship of thy tabrets and of thy pipes (music) was prepared in thee the day that thou wast created. Thou art the anointed cherub that covereth and I have set thee so, saith the Lord. Thou wast upon the holy mountain of God, thou hast walked up and down in the midst of the stones of fire."

As we go on, we realize he was perfect in all of his ways from the day he was created. With his tabrets and pipes, Lucifer not only was the "son of the morning" but he occupied the position as the heavenly leader of praise and worship. Tabrets and pipes indicate total concert of instruments and voices. (Guess who's taking his place now? You and me). What happened to the senior executive of total creation?

Let's examine this senior vice president, this creature, Lucifer. He was perfect in beauty, he had all the attributes that existed and exist today. The host of heaven looked up to him. He was assigned guardian of the throne of God (there were limited secrets that he was not apprised of), an anointed cherub, son of the morning, and possessed a position which, (as far as we know) was only lower than Elohim. No other anointed cherub or other angel in the hierarchy was "full of the sum" as was Lucifer. He was created perfect, the ultimate word in beauty (Colossians 1:16).

This made him proud. "I am just as perfect as Them," (the Trinity) are." He believed the lie and thus became the father of lies. A being of this stature, full of wisdom, had to have calculated this overthrow program of God, thinking he would be victorious. But he was deceived by pride, which he let breed in his mind and heart and it grew and manifested. Deception followed. He believed he could promote himself above God, "by terminating God's position through a democratic move. Majority rules. He apparently forgot that he was a creature, or a created being. Thus we have the first deception. Lucifer's ego deceived him. Watch your ego. He was given great wisdom, deep insight into the mystery of Elohim's creation. But God alone has knowledge of the beginning and the end. There could have been an area of directives that Lucifer found offensive. Now the RCP-1 theory is that when Elohim counseled on the creation of man (to be made in His own image) Lucifer became neurotic, and neurosis brings panic. Jealousy set in, thus his plan, believing that he would win by majority he became the first gambler and, as most gamblers, are deceived and lost. How could Lucifer believe he could de-throne Elohim? How could Lucifer believe he could de-throne the eternal God?

Chapter 9

Chapter Nine

The Choice of Angels

Lucifer saw God create. He knew the power of words and he shared in Elohim's counsel and had knowledge of some of the secrets of the universe. Let's go back to how he wagered on the outcome; that it would come out in his favor. After all, he was admired by the innumerable of the universe. Sound familiar? Do not take your eyes off God. One-third of the angels did. Many Christians today are admirers of and followers of a particular ministry and listen intently to every spoken word, as if it were dogma, better check it with the Word! Keep your eyes on Jesus.

Now Lucifer had the attention of all the angels and thus as we read Isaiah 14:13-14 we can create an image of a star war of the first kind. Lucifer hurled words into the universe on five different occasions as the angels and the Trinity looked on, knowing (deceived) that a majority of the angels would back him. As the powerful outcry of words, "I will ascend into heaven" (attempting to get the attention of all), "I will exalt my throne: (he did have a throne) "above the stars of God, I will sit upon the mount of the congregation, I will ascend above the heights of the clouds, I will be like the Most High," the Lord's reaction was immediate. He could have spoken one word and finalized the play, but He went through all the legal terms and as God spoke and said, "I will cast thee, Lucifer, as profane, out of the mountain of God." He also must have gone through a sad thought; God was sad, sorrowful, full of sorrow and grieving, as He said, "I will destroy thee, O covering cherub; I will cast thee to the ground, I will lay thee before kings." God said, "I will bring thee forth fire from the midst of thee which shall devour thee."

Lucifer is out of words, rebuked. Finally, God says, "I will bring thee to ashes upon the earth,," Ezekiel 28:16-18. The result of Lucifer's encounter; excommunication from that heaven, losing his first estate. Proverbs 1:18 tells us, "Pride goeth before destruction and a haughty spirit before a fall." Lucifer was lifted with pride. This encounter from the beginning of the deception could have taken place in a micro-second or within an hour, but not conceivably longer.

Being first to be deceived, and attempting to deceive, he was given many titles, one being "the master deceiver." As the initial deceived, liar, gambler, rebel against his Creator, he realized his master plan of tyranny had failed. Depending upon a majority of the angels to join in, Lucifer now has a new name, as God reveals His definitions into existence. The titles: accuser of the brethren, Satan, and the devil were branded on this rebellious creature, losing his name Lucifer, the light bearer, just as we find Elohim changing Abram's name to Abraham and Sarai's name to Sarah, taking the very breath of His name, Elohim and giving it to both Abraham and Sarah. Jacob's name was changed to Israel. Many of our names have been changed through Jesus to sons of God.

The first schism, Satan deceives and lives. Deception number two, it appears he has a great host of angelic partners. They were possibly in the billions. All of them were servants of God until deceived by the son of the morning. The Bible speaks of 10 thousands times 10 thousands and thousands of thousands. They are now deceiving millions of people on this earth. But we as alert believers, have the power of the Holy Spirit and the Word of God to resist this aggression.

When these angels and Satan rebelled, Elohim turned against them, due to the fact that their abilities would undermine the structure of the universe. Their ultimate punishment, along with those people who follow them, Jesus said, "Then shall he say also unto them on the left hand, depart from me ye cursed into everlasting fire, prepared for the devil and his angels" Matthew 25:41. Lucifer and his angels were cast out of their first estate, or out of the third heaven, and into the second estate, or the second heaven. Their powers were not all taken away but were simply reversed to evil, not reduced as some preach. However, Satan cannot have wisdom or love, because these are the attributes of the nature of God. And he has no power over the blood washed, Spirit-filled, praying believer

The Scripture, Ezekiel 28:12 speaks about the "iniquity of your traffic" in reference to Satan's deception of angels. Thus the second deception and a great multitude followed. So we have the first evil set forth in the universe, excelling itself. Unlike Satan who said, "I will exalt myself," we must come by way of the cross and humble ourselves in the sight of God and He will lift us up."

Praise God for His wisdom and love that He so graciously gives to those who are willing to become obedient to His voice and His Word. ☦

Made in the USA
Charleston, SC
21 July 2011